CANADA TURNS 150

CANADA
TODAY
2001-2017

Content Consultant:
David Mills, PhD, Retired Associate
Professor of Canadian History,
University of Alberta

BY ERIN NICKS

Published by Beech Street Books
27 Stewart Rd. Collingwood, ON Canada L9Y 4M7

www.beechstreetbooks.ca

Produced by Red Line Editorial

Photographs ©: Fred Chartrand/The Canadian Press/AP Images, cover, 1, 20; Art Babych/Shutterstock Images, 4, 24, 33; Sergei Bachlakov/Shutterstock Images, 5, 29; David P. Lewis/Shutterstock Images, 6; Government of Canada, 7; Dan Howell/Shutterstock Images, 8; Ryan Remiorz/The Canadian Press/AP Images, 9, 36; Chris So/Toronto Star/Getty Images, 11; NASA/Rex Features/AP Images, 13; Sean Kilpatrick/The Canadian Press/AP Images, 14; Stacey Newman/Shutterstock Images, 15; ValeStock/Shutterstock Images, 16; joseph s l tan matt/Shutterstock Images, 19; Frank Gunn/Canadian Press/AP Images, 23; Library and Archives Canada/PA-042133, 26–27; Department of Citizenship and Immigration-Information Division/Library and Archives Canada/PA-185533, 28; Larry MacDougal/The Canadian Press/AP Images, 30; Iurii Osadchi/Shutterstock Images, 31; arindambanerjee/Shutterstock Images, 32, 38; Jack Fordyce/Shutterstock Images, 34; Howard Sandler/Shutterstock Images, 35; Kathy Hutchins/Shutterstock Images, 37; Donny Ash/Shutterstock Images, 40–41; Serega/iStockphoto, 42

Editor: Alyssa Krekelberg
Designer: Laura Polzin and Mary Ross

Library and Archives Canada Cataloguing in Publication

Nicks, Erin, author
    Canada today 2001-2017 / by Erin Nicks.

 (Canada turns 150)
Includes bibliographical references and index.
Issued in print and electronic formats.
ISBN 978-1-77308-178-6 (hardcover).--ISBN 978-1-77308-269-1 (softcover).--
ISBN 978-1-77308-238-7 (PDF).--ISBN 978-1-77308-277-6 (HTML)

    1. Canada--History--21st century--Juvenile literature. 2. Canada--Social life and customs--21st century--Juvenile literature. 3. Canada--Civilization--21st century--Juvenile literature. I. Title.

FC640.N54 2017   j971.07   C2017-903685-8
                                                       C2017-903686-6

Printed in the United States of America
Mankato, MN
August 2017

TABLE OF CONTENTS

CANADA
TODAY (2001–2017)

A Time of Great Change

Throughout the 2000s, events both difficult and exciting helped shape modern-day Canada. Over the years the Canadian community came together and became stronger than ever before. Canadians sheltered stranded Americans after a terrorist attack. They laughed and cried over films led by brilliant Canadian directors. And the Canadian people prepared to celebrate their nation's 150th anniversary.

The government played a large role in many events throughout this time period. Beginning in 2000, government leadership swung three times. The Liberals dominated Parliament through the early part of the decade. Then the Conservatives gained control. By 2015 the nation was ready for another change.

Justin Trudeau was elected prime minister in 2015.

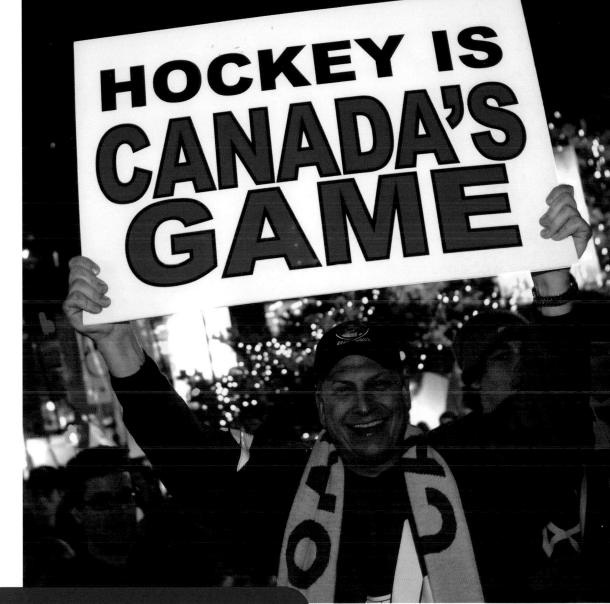

Canadians celebrated after their hockey teams won gold medals at the 2010 Winter Olympic Games.

The election of Liberal prime minister Justin Trudeau created a stir around the world. As the son of former prime minister Pierre Trudeau, he had big shoes to fill.

At the same time, people across Canada cheered for their beloved sports teams. Canadian hockey teams continued to garner international attention throughout the start of this century. The women's hockey team won its first gold medal at the Salt Lake City Olympics

People across the country celebrate their nation on Canada Day.

in 2002. The city of Vancouver hosted the historic Winter Games in 2010, where both the men's and women's hockey teams won gold.

This was also a time when people across Canada fought for human rights and social issues. In 2005 Canada legalized same-sex marriage. In addition, **Indigenous** rights became a regular point of discussion. In 2008 Prime Minister Stephen Harper formally apologized for generations of abuse that Indigenous children suffered at residential schools. Additionally, years later the Supreme Court ruled that North America's first legal drug injection site would remain open.

As the Canadian people celebrated their country's 150-year anniversary in 2017, they looked back on the events that helped shape Canada. In addition, they looked toward the bright future with excitement and resolve to make the next century even more spectacular.

CANADA 150

Operation Yellow Ribbon

On September 11, 2001, four US airplanes were **hijacked** by members of the radicalized Islamic terrorist group Al-Qaeda. Two planes were flown into skyscrapers in New York City, New York. One struck a government building outside Washington, DC. The last plane crashed in a Pennsylvania field. More than 2,900 people died, including 26 Canadians.

Immediately after the attacks, airports across the United States shut down. However, many airplanes heading to American cities were still in the air. After the terrorist attacks, the Canadian government organized a plan named Operation Yellow Ribbon. The plan redirected planes to safe places to land at airports within Canada. Over 200 airplanes from around the world arrived safely on Canadian soil. Moncton, St. John's, Halifax, Montréal, Toronto, Winnipeg, Calgary, and Vancouver all saw the arrival of planes originally destined for the United States.

The World Trade Center towers collapsed less than two hours after being struck.

Find a related web link at **canada150.beechstreetbooks.ca**.

In 2011 Gander held a memorial ceremony for victims of the 9/11 attacks.

Did You Know?

Thirty-eight flights holding 6,656 people landed in Gander, Newfoundland, on September 11, 2001. The residents opened their homes to the stranded passengers. They gave them shelter until US airports reopened later that week. A Broadway musical *Come From Away* was created based on the event. Each year the town holds ceremonies of remembrance for the September 11 anniversary.

?

HELPING
FORGOTTEN ANIMALS

Bonnie Harris Cares for Animals Left on Planes after 9/11

Bonnie Harris was working at the Gander animal shelter when planes began landing in the Newfoundland town. Harris felt certain that with so many aircraft landing in Gander, it was likely that at least some were carrying animals. At night she would try to sleep but was overwhelmed with thoughts of pets left abandoned on the planes. Had anyone bothered to check, or had they been too overwhelmed with the stress and magnitude of the event? She called the ground crews working at the airport where the planes were held and asked if there had been animals on the planes. Her hunch was correct. Many animals were listed as being on board. When she inquired if anyone had made arrangements for food or care, the answer was no. That was all Harris needed to hear. After receiving permission from local authorities, she decided to go from plane to plane, searching for animals that had been left behind. Crawling in the bellies of the aircraft, she found cats, dogs, and even a pair of endangered apes in cages on the airplanes. Some of the animals needed medicine, and all needed attention.

Bonnie Harris poses with photos of the chimpanzees that she rescued from an American airplane on 9/11.

Harris and her assistant loaded a truck with pet food, water, medicine, and other supplies from their shelter. They began going from cage to cage, feeding and treating the animals. It was hard work. Harris wanted to remove the pets from the airplanes. She called Dr. Doug Tweedie, a government regional veterinarian. With his help they received permission to get the animals off the airplanes. The pets were taken to an empty airplane hangar where Harris could take care of them properly.

First Canadian to Walk in Space

Chris Hadfield, an astronaut from southern Ontario, became the first Canadian to walk in space in 2001. Hadfield joined the Canadian Armed Forces in 1978 and eventually began training as a fighter pilot. His hard work paid off, and he began to fly aircraft for the North American Aerospace Defence Command.

In 1992 more than 5,000 people applied to become a Canadian astronaut. Hadfield was chosen as one of four astronauts that year. The Canadian Space Agency (CSA) told him to pack his bags and head to Houston, Texas, to work at the NASA Johnson Space Center. Hadfield used his experience and degree in mechanical engineering to help NASA with safety and technical issues, shuttle launches, and the development of a glass shuttle cockpit.

November 1995 was Hadfield's first mission into space. He served as a mission specialist for the crew of space shuttle *Atlantis*. Over the years, Hadfield made it to orbit three times. In 2013 Hadfield decided to retire from the CSA after a long, prosperous career.

"It's interesting to wake up one day and know that you're going to ride a rocket to space that day." (Chris Hadfield)

Did You Know?

Chris Hadfield has flown more than 70 different kinds of aircraft.

?

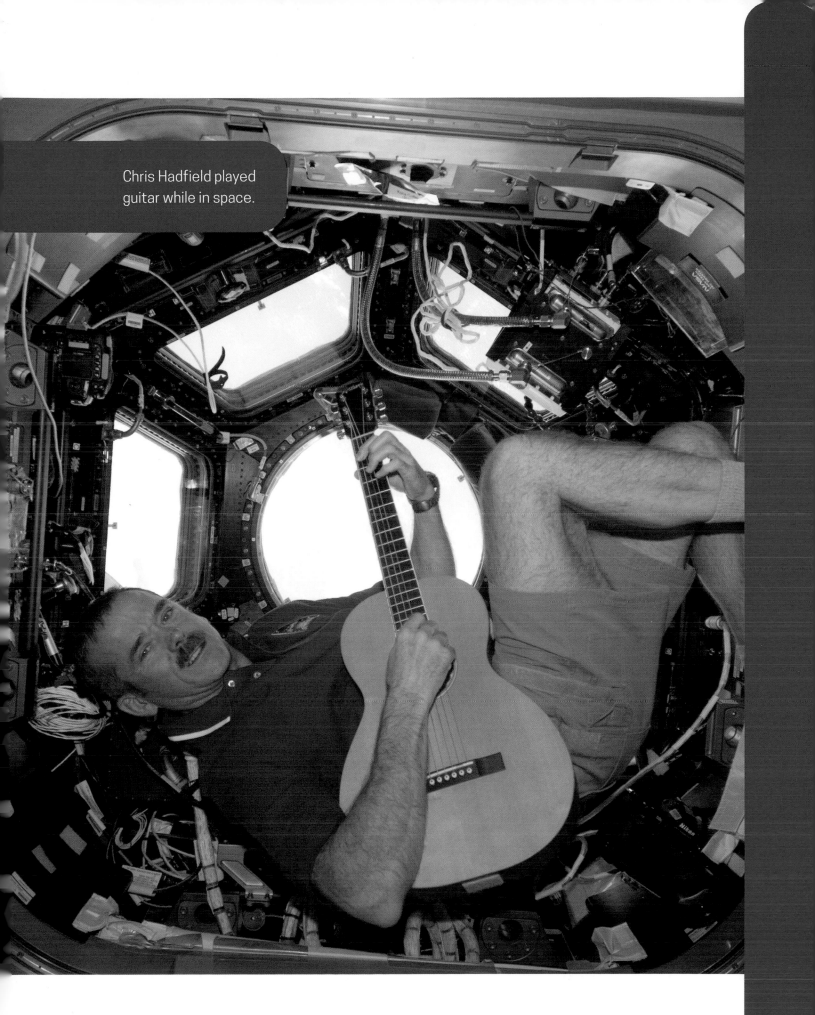

Chris Hadfield played guitar while in space.

Operation Apollo

In 2001 after the United States began targeting the terrorist group Al-Qaeda in Afghanistan, Canada announced that it would provide sea, land, and air forces to the fight. The operation was named Apollo. Roughly 2,000 men and women served in the mission. Apollo ended in 2003, with some of its military members coming back to Canada. Others went on to serve in other missions, such as Operation Athena and Operation Attention, until Canada ended its formal operations in Afghanistan in 2014.

Immigration Influx

In the 1990s the government opened the doors to more immigrants from Asia and the Middle East than ever before. The percentage of Canadian residents born outside Canada reached its highest level in 70 years. In 2001, immigrants made up more than 18 percent of the population. The number of foreign-born people in Canada was second only to Australia. An increase in immigration changed the face of Canada. Today this **multiculturalism** is an important part of the Canadian identity.

Canadians welcomed Syrian refugees in 2015.

Canada Leads Kyoto Charge

Canada was one of the first countries to sign the Kyoto Protocol in 1998. The Protocol is an international treaty created to reduce **greenhouse gases** around the world. It took four years for all the countries involved to negotiate and agree upon the cuts that needed to be made to their pollution levels. In December 2002, Canada **ratified** its participation in the treaty. The deal committed Canada and 36 other countries to cut their carbon emissions to help fight climate change.

One source of greenhouse gases comes from burning fossil fuels for cars.

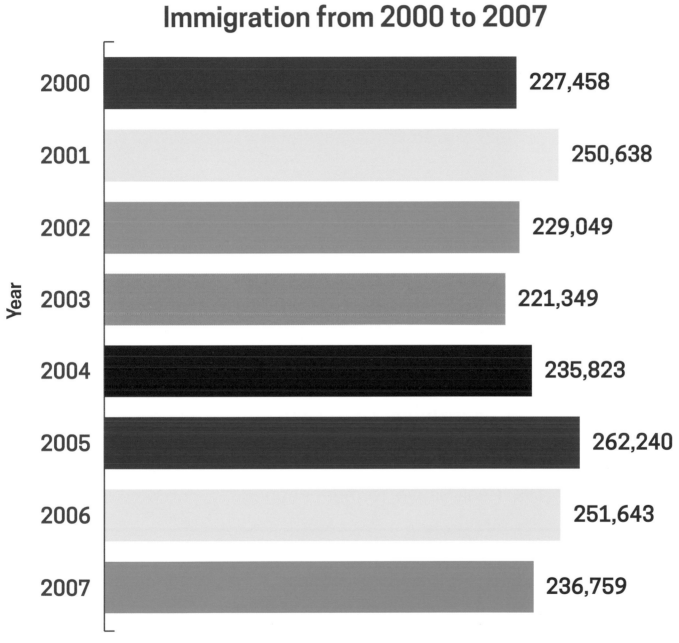

Immigration from 2000 to 2007

Year	Number of Immigrants
2000	227,458
2001	250,638
2002	229,049
2003	221,349
2004	235,823
2005	262,240
2006	251,643
2007	236,759

Mi-Jung Lee

TV broadcaster Mi-Jung Lee is one of Canada's most recognized Korean immigrants. She served as a television anchor and producer of *CTV News* from 2001 to 2010. Lee was four years old when she moved to Vancouver from South Korea in the 1970s. Lee noted that when her family moved to Canada, the standards of life weren't great in South Korea. Her parents wanted to build a better life for their daughters.

Growing up, Lee watched her parents overcome obstacles to create a new life. "I learned from them how important it is to persevere through difficult situations," she said.

Prisoners Allowed to Vote

For years Canadian prisoners were banned from voting in elections. However, in 2002 the Supreme Court ruled that preventing prisoners from voting was a violation of fundamental rights.

> "I just couldn't understand. I never lost my citizenship—I was still a citizen. It was clear to me that the Charter [of Rights and Freedoms] said that I still had the right to vote."
> (Rick Sauvé, former prisoner)

Rick Sauvé

Rick Sauvé was convicted of first-degree murder in 1979. In 1984 after being sent to prison, Sauvé challenged his lack of voting rights. This turned into a 20-year legal journey to the Supreme Court. The Supreme Court's ruling in 2002 ensured that all persons, even prisoners, could vote. Sauvé was released on parole after serving 17 years. He now works with a volunteer program, counselling inmates who are serving life sentences.

National Aboriginal Day is celebrated annually on June 21.

Celebrating Diversity

In 2002, the government proclaimed June 27 as Canadian Multiculturalism Day. People across Canada celebrate the country's diversity and show appreciation to the many cultural groups that call Canada home.

On a raison de dire

NON

On a raison de dire NON

LA S...A NON ...RATION?

Québec Liberal leader Daniel Johnson gave a victory speech after the Québec referendum votes were counted.

Sponsorship Scandal

In October 1995, Québec held a vote to decide if it should leave Canada and become an independent country. The vote was close, but in the end 50.6 percent of Québec's voting residents chose to remain a part of Canada. However, nearly half the people living in the province still felt they should become independent.

After the vote, the Liberal government secretly paid communications companies to raise Canada's profile in Québec. These companies received $100 million from the government to sponsor events and purchase new technology for Québec institutions, all in the name of Canada. The money was to be used to highlight Canada as a sponsor for certain events.

These sponsorships were supposed to help the residents of Québec associate Canada with happier events in their province.

However, the money wasn't being used correctly. Communications companies paid their employees with government money. Allegations of fraud were made in 2002, and the media exposed this deal in 2003. An investigation was conducted by the auditor general. This scandal caused the Liberals to lose their majority in Parliament during the 2004 election. Voters were upset with how their tax dollars had been misused.

"I am deeply disturbed that such practices were allowed to happen in the first place. I don't think anybody can take this lightly." (Federal auditor general Sheila Fraser on the Liberal sponsorship scandal, 2004)

Women's Hockey Wins Gold

The women representing Canada's hockey team slid onto the ice. They were at the 2002 Winter Olympics in Salt Lake City, Utah, and were prepared to face Team USA for the gold medal. Cheers erupted from the stands as the teams waited for the puck to drop. Canada had lost the gold medal to the United States in the 1998 Winter Olympics, and the team was ready to redeem itself. Caroline Ouellette, Hayley Wickenheiser, and Jayna Hefford sealed the win for Team Canada, bringing the final score to 3–2.

> "It's been four long years thinking about that disappointment in '98 and finally bringing the gold medal home to the country where it belongs." (Team Canada captain Cassie Campbell, 2002)

BlackBerry Smart Phone

BlackBerry, based in Waterloo, Ontario, established itself in the phone business after it released its first product in 1999. As the phones evolved over time, they kept their sleek-looking physical keyboard that consumers loved. In 2003 the phones boasted modern features such as web browsing capability and email access. ⌒⊃

Did You Know?

The first same-sex marriage in Canada occurred on June 10, 2003, when Michael Leshner and Michael Stark wed in Toronto. One week later, Prime Minister Jean Chrétien introduced legislation that would legalize same-sex marriage.

?

Canada Legalizes Same-Sex Marriage

A bill passed by the House of Commons in June 2005 granted gay and lesbian couples the right to marry. Before the federal law came into place one month later, same-sex marriages were not recognized in the Northwest Territories, Nunavut, Alberta, and Prince Edward Island. Canada was the fourth country in the world to legally recognize same-sex marriage throughout its borders.

Michael Leshner, *left*, and Michael Stark, *centre*, sign their marriage certificate in 2003. They were married by Superior Court Justice John Hamilton, *right*.

Kelowna Accord

The 2005 Kelowna Accord was a 10-year plan designed to help strengthen the relationship between Indigenous Peoples and the government. Both parties wanted to improve education, health, housing, and economic opportunities in all the Indigenous communities. The cost to improve these things was estimated at $5 billion. Prime Minister Paul Martin of the Liberal government agreed to these terms. However, the Conservative administration took power in 2006 and cut funding for this program. Prime Minister Stephen Harper claimed that the Accord was too ambitious and expensive to activate.

"Had the [Kelowna] Accord been honoured, I believe we would have lived a very different decade. But since 2006, too little has changed—unfairness was allowed to persist, and time marched on." (former prime minister Paul Martin, May 11, 2016)

Stephen Harper served as prime minister from 2006 to 2015.

Montréal Expos Play Last Game

In 2004 the Montréal Expos baseball team played its last home game before moving to Washington, DC. Approximately 31,000 fans filled the stadium to watch the Expos, who ultimately lost the game to the Florida Marlins. The next season the Expos' name changed to the Nationals. The team has been in Washington, DC, ever since.

Residential School Abuse

On June 11, 2008, Prime Minister Stephen Harper formally apologized to Indigenous Peoples for the Indian residential schools system. For more than a century the Government of Canada had separated more than 150,000 Indigenous children from their homes and families. The government had tried to **assimilate** them into the white culture. In these schools many children were abused and neglected. Residential schools helped destroy generations of First Nations cultures. The schools forced children to speak English instead of their Indigenous languages. They also changed their Indigenous names to English versions, and banned them from any other First Nations cultural practices, such as ceremonial dances used to celebrate nature.⊂∞

⊂∞ Find a related web link at **canada150.beechstreetbooks.ca**.

Indigenous children were forced to experience a European classroom-style education.

"Two primary objectives of the Residential Schools system were to remove and isolate children from the influence of their homes, families, traditions, and cultures and to assimilate them into the dominant culture. These objectives were based on the assumption Aboriginal cultures and spiritual beliefs were inferior and unequal. . . . Today, we recognize that this policy of assimilation was wrong, has caused great harm, and has no place in our country." (Prime Minister Stephen Harper, 2008)

Basil Ambers

Basil Ambers is a member of the Kwakwaka'wakw First Nation. As a child he was forced to attend St. Michael's Indian Residential School in Alert Bay, British Columbia. St. Michael's operated from 1929 to 1975. Years later, Ambers reflected on what life was like in the St. Michael's school system: "We were hungry constantly. I became a table captain, so I had to dish out the food to the kids at my table. Quite often I never got enough to eat myself because I ended up giving too much to one or two of the kids. . . . For breakfast we had porridge, but there were maggots in the porridge. We used to kid each other about having iron to supplement the porridge."

Winter Olympics on the West Coast

Vancouver was the host city for the 2010 Winter Olympics. Nearly 2,600 athletes from 82 countries participated in the games. Canada won 14 gold medals. This was the most gold medals ever won by a single country at a Winter Olympics. The total medal count for Canada was 26. It was a record high for the nation! ⊖⊃

Vancouver's Olympic Cauldron

The Red Mitten

The Canadian athletes wore red mittens featuring a white maple leaf on the palms during the opening ceremonies in the 2010 Winter Olympics. The mittens were created by Hudson's Bay Company. They were a last-minute addition to the torch-bearer's uniform. After the ceremonies the public demand to buy these mittens was overwhelming. Stores began to stock them. More than 3 million sets were sold.

The iconic red mittens of the 2010 Winter Olympics

Hayley Wickenheiser

Hayley Wickenheiser was one of the best female hockey players in the world. She is a five-time Olympic medalist. Wickenheiser helped lead the Canadian hockey team to the gold medal in the 2002 Winter Olympics. She added three more Olympic gold medals to her collection while in Turin, Italy, in 2006; Vancouver in 2010; and Sochi, Russia, in 2014.

Wickenheiser wanted to play on a bigger ice surface. To accomplish her goal, she had to start trying out for men's leagues, and the Finnish Hockey Federation was happy to allow her to play. In 2003 Wickenheiser became the first woman in history to score a point in a men's professional game. She recorded an assist while playing with Kirkkonummen Salamat of the Finnish second division. After 23 years on the Canadian women's team, Wickenheiser retired from hockey in 2017.

Rallies were held in Toronto to raise awareness about climate change.

Canada Withdraws from Kyoto Protocol

Prime Minister Stephen Harper withdrew from the Kyoto Protocol in 2011. The protocol had asked countries to provide financial support to other developing nations in the hopes that they could fight climate change. Harper blamed the country's economic downturn, stating that Canada did not have the funds to make the required cuts or provide assistance.

Supreme Court Keeps Legal Injection Site Open

Insite in Vancouver is North America's first supervised legal injection site. The location gives people with drug addictions the ability to administer illegal intravenous drugs in a safe, clean environment. This led to fewer drug **overdoses** in the community. However, Prime Minister Stephen Harper was opposed to this facility and wanted it closed. Harper and the Conservative government believed the system should be focused on preventing people from becoming addicted to drugs. In 2011 the Supreme Court ruled that the site would remain open. The court said that not allowing Insite to operate was a violation of the Charter of Rights and Freedoms.

The Supreme Court building was designed by Montréal architect Ernest Cormier.

Rise of Canadian Music

Canada is home to international superstars who specialize in a variety of different music genres, such as rapper Drake, pop singer Justin Bieber, and alternative R&B artist Abel Tesfaye, known by his stage name, The Weeknd.

Drake's rise to fame began in 2001, when he joined the television show *Degrassi: The Next Generation*. Years later, in 2006, the Toronto native made an attempt to break into the music scene by releasing his first mixtape, *Room for Improvement*. He continued making music and in 2016 was named by *Forbes* magazine as one of the wealthiest hip-hop artists.

Bieber was born in London, Ontario. He skyrocketed to stardom in 2009 after he released his first single, "One Time." The song went platinum in Canada and the United States. Since then, Bieber has released a number of popular albums.

The Weeknd is from Toronto and is known across Canada and the United States. He made headlines in the music industry after releasing his tape *House of Balloons* in 2011. Two years later, The Weeknd won the Juno Award for Breakthrough Artist of the Year.

Justin Bieber

Jack Layton

Jack Layton served as the leader of the New Democratic Party from 2003 to 2011. The party grew under his leadership from 13 members of Parliament to 103. A growing number of Canadians were unhappy with the Liberals. However, they were unwilling to support the Conservatives. Many people began to side with Layton and the New Democratic Party. Layton wanted to increase funding for health and social assistance programs. He also wanted to improve public transportation and focus on the environment. At the height of his political success and popularity with the Canadian people, Layton was diagnosed with cancer. He died in 2011 at the age of 61.

Jack Layton
(1950–2011)

"My friends, love is better than anger. Hope is better than fear. Optimism is better than despair. So let us be loving, hopeful, and optimistic. And we'll change the world."
(Jack Layton)

Lac-Mégantic Rail Disaster

On the night of July 5, 2013, a train from North Dakota in the United States was bound for New Brunswick. It was carrying more than 7 million litres of **crude oil**. After stopping in Québec, a fire broke out on the train. The fire was extinguished, but it caused the train's brakes to fail. The train rolled downhill toward the town of Lac-Mégantic. It derailed near the town centre, and about 6 million litres of oil was released and caught fire. Many residents had no time to react before the train burst into a massive fireball. The blaze and explosions killed 47 people. Approximately 2,000 people were forced from their homes.

Did You Know?

After the Lac-Mégantic disaster 169 people became homeless, 27 children were orphaned, and 44 buildings were destroyed.

Québec Filmmakers Continue to Dominate Industry

French Canadian filmmakers made headlines outside Canada during this decade. Jean-Marc Vallée directed actors Matthew McConaughey and Jared Leto in *Dallas Buyers Club*. Both actors went on to win Oscars for those roles in 2014, while Vallée was nominated for his work behind the camera. He also directed Reese Witherspoon in *Wild*. Denis Villeneuve directed Jake Gyllenhaal in *Prisoners* and *Enemy*. He was nominated for an Oscar for *Arrival* in 2017. Xavier Dolan won the Grand Prix at the Cannes Film Festival for *It's Only the End of the World* in 2016.

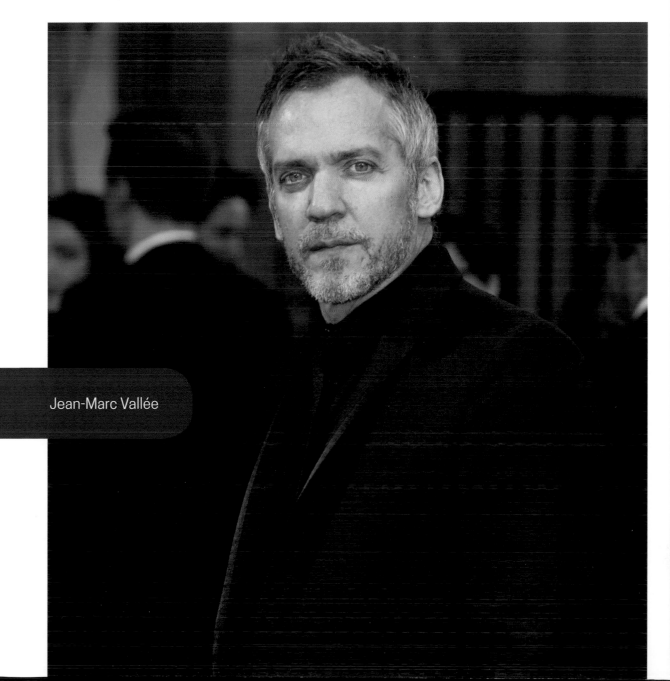

Jean-Marc Vallée

Military Operations End

Canadian forces spent 12 years battling Al-Qaeda in Afghanistan. In 2014 officials lowered the Canadian flag at the North Atlantic Treaty Organization (NATO) headquarters in Kabul, Afghanistan. Twenty-eight countries are part of NATO. Its purpose is to safeguard the freedom and security of its members through political and military means. The lowering of the flag signalled the formal end of Canada's military operations in Afghanistan.

Did You Know?

Between 2002 and 2011 more than 160 Canadians were killed during the military operation in Afghanistan, including 158 soldiers, 1 diplomat, 1 journalist, and 2 civilian contractors. More than 2,000 Canadian soldiers were also wounded during this period.

Justin Trudeau Leads Liberals

Justin Trudeau, son of former prime minister Pierre Trudeau, was elected as the 23rd prime minister of Canada on October 19, 2015. Trudeau had served as the head of the Liberal Party since 2013. He achieved a majority government and secured seats in every province and territory. Trudeau made international headlines by appointing an equal number of men and women to his **cabinet**. The move signalled a step forward for gender equality. It was the first cabinet of its kind in Canadian history.

Justin Trudeau at an election rally in 2015

Real Change Now
Changer ensemble maintenant

FOR A BETTER ECONOMY

The wildfire in Alberta was the largest fire evacuation in the province's history.

Wildfire Chaos in Alberta

In May 2016, a wildfire—likely started by human activity—began in northeastern Alberta and spread to Fort McMurray. Nearly 90,000 people were evacuated from Fort McMurray and the surrounding areas. Residents recorded videos as they left. The videos showed the fire came very close to the highway. Many fleeing residents were only metres away from the fire when they drove past. Approximately 2,400 homes and buildings were destroyed. However, no deaths were directly caused by the fire.

Did You Know?

At its largest point, the wildfire spread to over 500,000 **hectares**. This is an area larger than Prince Edward Island.

"At one point, I couldn't cry (if I wanted to). I had 40 years of stuff in that house." (Tamara Wolfe, resident of Fort McMurray)

Fireworks on Parliament Hill

Canada Celebrates 150 Years

The year 2017 marked Canada's 150th year as a united nation. Plans began several years in advance for this celebratory occasion. Cultural, music, and sporting events took place across the country throughout the entire year. As the capital city, Ottawa prepared to take centre stage for many celebrations. The city focused on commemorating Canada's multicultural heritage. Canada invited the embassies and high commissions from other countries to mark their own national celebration in Ottawa throughout 2017. By doing this, Canada hoped to strengthen its ties with other countries and promote unity around the world.

Did You Know?

- More than 36 million people lived in Canada at the start of 2017.
- English and French are the country's official languages.
- At least 65 Indigenous groups live in Canada.
- Canadian inventions include basketball, snowmobiles, electric wheelchairs, and peanut butter.

"When we celebrate Canada 150, we celebrate generations of Canadians who sought common ground so we could share a common, more hopeful future. For 150 years Canada has been a success story, but that will only continue with a lot of hard work." (Prime Minister Justin Trudeau, 2017)

TIMELINE

2001: Operation Yellow Ribbon is created; Chris Hadfield is the first Canadian to walk in space; Canada announces it will send troops to Afghanistan; immigrants make up more than 18 percent of Canada's population.

2002: The Kyoto Accord is ratified by Canada; Canadian prisoners receive the right to vote; Canadian Multiculturalism Day is proclaimed as June 27.

2003: Liberal sponsorship scandal occurs; BlackBerry releases smart phone.

2005: Same-sex marriage is made legal across Canada.

2006: Stephen Harper becomes prime minister; funding is cut for the Kelowna Accord.

2008: Prime Minister Stephen Harper formally apologizes for residential schools.

2010: The Winter Olympics take place in Vancouver; red mittens worn by Canadian Olympians are sold in stores.

2011: Canada withdraws from the Kyoto Protocol; Supreme Court keeps Insite open; Canadian musicians continue to gain popularity.

2013: Lac-Mégantic rail disaster occurs.

2014: French Canadian filmmakers gain international attention; the Canadian flag is lowered in Kabul as Canadian operations cease in Afghanistan.

2015: Justin Trudeau is elected as prime minister.

2016: Alberta wildfires occur.

2017: Canada celebrates 150 years as a nation.

GLOSSARY

ASSIMILATE

to take the cultural traditions of a population

CABINET

the group of ministers who work closely with the prime minister

CRUDE OIL

petroleum as it comes from an oil well or after substances (water, gas, and minerals) are removed

GREENHOUSE GASES

gases that cause air pollution, which leads to climate change

HECTARES

hectares are a unit of measurement; one hectare is the equivalent of 10,000 square metres

HIJACKED

to have taken over a vehicle, such as an airplane, especially through force

INDIGENOUS

originating in a certain place

MULTICULTURALISM

diverse cultures within a society

OVERDOSES

dangerous amounts of drug dosage that can be lethal

RATIFIED

approved or consented to a treaty, contract, or formal agreement

TO LEARN MORE

BOOKS

Jones, Molly. *Relationships with Aboriginal First Nations*. Collingwood, ON: Beech Street Books, 2017.

Littlechild, George. *The Spirit Giggles Within*. Victoria, BC: Heritage, 2012.

Morrison, Jennifer. *Wayne Gretzky: Greatness on Ice*. St. Catharines, ON: Crabtree, 2011.

WEBSITES

Canada Country Profile
http://kids.nationalgeographic.com/explore/countries/canada/#canada-playing-hockey.jpg

The Changing Face of Canadian Immigration in One Chart
http://www.macleans.ca/news/canada/the-changing-face-of-canadian-immigration-in-one-chart

A History of Residential Schools in Canada
http://www.cbc.ca/news/canada/a-history-of-residential-schools-in-canada-1.702280

INDEX

ABOUT THE AUTHOR

Erin Nicks is from Thunder Bay, Ontario. She has worked as a writer, newspaper columnist, and reporter for nearly 20 years. She currently resides in Ottawa, Ontario.